Tween Friends

Jewelry & Accessories

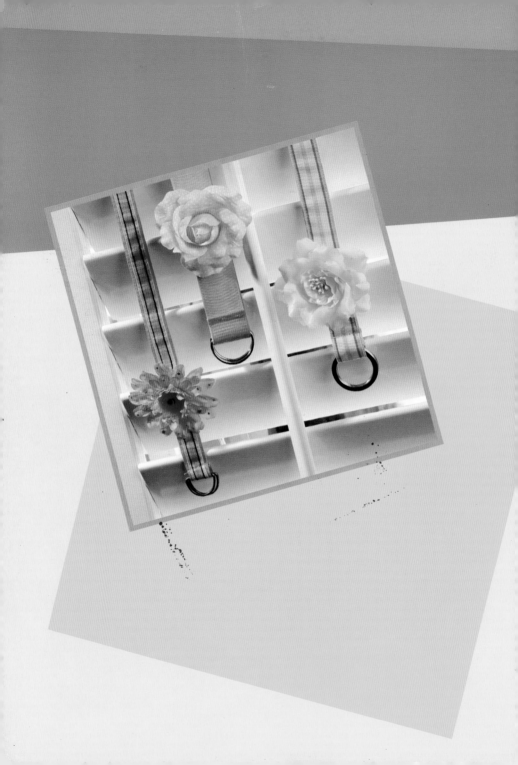

Tween Friends

Jewelry & Accessories

Jill Williams Grover

Sterling Publishing Co., Inc. New York
A Sterling/Chapelle Book

Chapelle, Ltd., Inc., P.O. Box 9252, Ogden, UT 84409
  (801) 621-2777 • (801) 621-2788 Fax
  e-mail: chapelle@chapelleltd.com
  Web site: www.chapelleltd.com

Space would not permit the inclusion of every decorative item photographed for this book, nor could all of the designers be identified. Many of these items are available by contacting:
  Ruby & Begonia, 204 25th Street, Ogden, UT 84401
  (801) 334-7829 • (888) 888-7829 Toll-free
  e-mail: ruby@rubyandbegonia.com
  Web site: www.rubyandbegonia.com

Every effort has been made to ensure that all information in this book is accurate. However, due to differing conditions, tools, and individual skills, the publisher cannot be responsible for any injuries, losses, and/or other damages which may result from the use of the information in this book.

This volume is meant to stimulate craft ideas. If readers are unfamiliar or not proficient in a skill necessary to attempt a project, we urge that they refer to an instructional book specifically addressing the required technique.

Library of Congress Cataloging-in-Publication Data available
Grover, Jill Williams.
  Tween friends jewelry & accessories / Jill Williams Grover.
    p. cm.
  Includes index.
  ISBN 1-4027-1326-6
  1. Handicraft for girls. 2. Jewelry making. 3. Dress accessories. I. Title.
  TT171.G693 2005
  745.5--dc22

                                                                    2005003998

  10 9 8 7 6 5 4 3 2 1
  Published by Sterling Publishing Co., Inc.
  387 Park Avenue South, New York, NY 10016
  ©2005 by Jill Williams Grover
  Distributed in Canada by Sterling Publishing
  c/o Canadian Manda Group, 165 Dufferin Street
  Toronto, Ontario, Canada M6K 3H6
  Distributed in Great Britain by Chrysalis Books Group PLC,
The Chrysalis Building,
Bramley Road, London W10 6SP, England
Distributed in Australia by Capricorn Link (Australia) Pty. Ltd.
P. O. Box 704, Windsor, NSW 2756, Australia
Printed and Bound in China
All Rights Reserved

Sterling ISBN 1-4027-1326-6

For information about custom editions, special sales, premium and corporate purchases, please contact Sterling Special Sales Department at 800-805-5489 or specialsales@sterlingpub.com

Contents

Flower Power

Flower Design Bag

Add flower embellishments of your choice to any bag using fabric glue. Cut a simple flower shape from felt or from a desired fabric, then attach to the bag. You could also attach purchased flower appliqués.

You could also attach a flower to a hair band.

Purchase a chain belt and attach a flower pin. You can wear this as a belt or necklace.

Hat Cover

Attach one or more flowers to a hat. You can either pin the flowers or glue the flowers to the hat with fabric glue. It would be nice to add the same touch to a matching scarf.

SECRET

Make an adorable ring by attaching a flower. You choose the size of the flower—be bold!

Flower That Purse

Use hot glue or fabric glue to cover an entire purse with flowers, or simply add one flower.

Scarf It

Attach a flower pin to a scarf to make a belt or to wear around your neck.

Ribbon Wrap

Purchase a ribbon belt or make your own.
Now attach a flower pin. This is such a simple
accessory to make, but it really makes a great fashion
statement–especially when worn with a pair of jeans.

Flowery Pearls

SECRET

For fun, pin a flower to your lapel. Accessorize with more than one flower if you feel like it; the idea works best if you use different shapes and sizes.

Attach a purchased flower to a pearl necklace. You could also substitute the flower for a ribbon tied in a bow.

Black Ribbon Beauty

Cut a flower shape from your favorite
color of felt. Attach the flower to a black
ribbon, using fabric glue. This project can be
used for a necklace, bracelet, ankle bracelet, or hair
ribbon. You could even make a row of flowers.

Rose Ties

1a

1b

1c

1d

Select a fun man's tie and cut in half. Each tie will make two rose pins (see diagram 1a). Roll the tie into a spiral for 4" (see diagram 1b). Twist the rest of the tie and wrap around the spiral (see diagram 1c). Place a straight ball pin to hold in place (see diagram 1d). Cut a round felt piece and hot glue to bottom of the flower. Hot glue a safety pin to the felt piece.

Girlie Girl

Splashy Rubber Gloves

Gussy up a
pair of rubber
gloves by adding
ribbon, flowers,
trim, and lace.
Washing the dishes
will never be the
same again. This is a
great gift idea for your
girlie girlfriend.

Boyfriend Required Purse

Find a zipper pull with your
boyfriend or another friend's name.
Attach it to your purse with a ribbon.
Another fun idea would be to attach this
zipper pull to your belt buckle.

Wildly Fun Winter Scarves

Use a clever napkin ring as a scarf ring. Scarves aren't just outerwear anymore; feel free to wear one indoors with a simple knit top.

Charmed Circle

Attach a wine charm ring to a purchased colorful bangle bracelet. If you can't find wine charms, you could use tiny ring earrings.

Cheery Clutch Bag

Create a clutch bag by using a fabric hot pad. First make three folds (see diagram 1a). Sew a seam on each side or, if you prefer, use fabric glue. Add trim or a vintage pin (see diagram 1b-c). Also shown is a cute purse made by sewing or gluing two hot pads together (see diagram 2). Add ribbon or pearls to make the purse strap.

1a

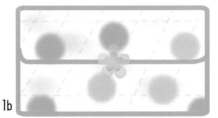

1b

2

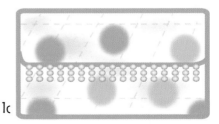

1c

Grasping
a clutch bag
is a graceful,
feminine gesture.

SECRET

Crystal Jewelry

Bracelet:

To make the bracelet you will need one
12" stretch string, about 50 Swarovski crystal beads, and a
dab of glue to seal the knot.

Tie one end of the elastic string with a knot and string on the
beads. Tie the ends together with a square not (right over left, left
over right) and put a small dab of glue on the knot. Let dry. Trim
off any excess string.

Earrings:

For the earrings you will need two head pins, 12 Swarovski crystal beads, two ear wires or studs, round nose pliers, and wire cutters. Thread 6 beads onto each head pin. Take one head pin and use round nose pliers to roll the excess wire down into a small circle. (Always roll away from yourself.) Trim the wire, if necessary. Attach the ear wires or studs by gently pulling the small loop apart. Place the head pin circle in the ear wire or stud and close.

Necklace:

To make the necklace you will need about 120 Swarovski crystals (or desired length), 2" of 25 lb. fishing line, two clam shells, one clasp, and pliers. Tie a knot in one end of the fishing line. Add one of the clam shells to cover the knot and gently close it with the pliers. String the beads. Place the other clam shell on so that its back is to the crystal beads. Tie the fishing line off close to the clam shell. Attach the clasp by closing the tail of the clam shell around the small ring on the clasp. Repeat with other side.

Curtain Jewelry

Purchase any curtain jewelry that you love. You can make great neckware and belts.

Curtain jewelry is usually less expensive than buying costume jewelry. Be creative. I like this idea because then you have a one-of-a-kind jewelry item, not just one off the rack like everyone else.

Wire Word Bracelets

You
can find
great ideas
for jewelry at
any scrapbooking
store.

Purchase scrapbooking words and
attach them to wire. Attach the
wire to fit your wrist.

Classy Initial Clutch Bags

Attach a name or initial to a clutch bag by using scrapbooking letters.

Lacy Waist Wrap

Make a great waist wrap from a thrift-store curtain valance. Just add ribbon to the ends to make the tie.

I saw a celebrity wearing something like this. You can get great inspiration from the famous people because they wear the latest and greatest.

Friendship Rings

Cut a ponytail holder (see diagram 1a). Pull both ends of the ponytail holder through a charm that has a hole in the center; adjust to fit (see diagram 1b-c). It's a good idea to add a drop of fabric glue to the center to keep the ponytail holder from pulling out.

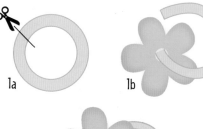

1a

1b

1c

Winter Wise

Embellish a purchased hat and scarf
by simply tying random ribbon bows.

Fun

Knotty Jewelry

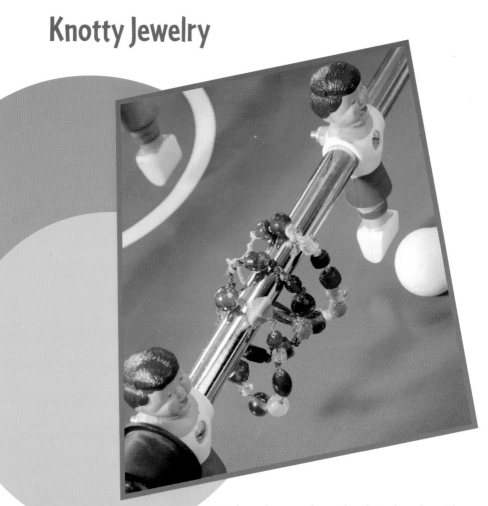

Make a knotty bracelet, hair band, ankle bracelet, a tie for a backpack, or a key ring. Cut a piece of hemp at least 18" long. Tie a double knot 2" from one end. Dab a bit of glue at the other end and twist into a point (the hardened tip will make the stringing of beads easy to do). Let dry. String the beads onto the hemp. Make a double knot after you add each bead. Repeat to desired length.

Tie Belt

Use a man's tie for a belt, a hair band, or even a scarf. For fun, you could wear it the masculine way, around your neck. Thrift stores are a great source for this accessory.

Cat & Dog Collars

Go to a pet store and purchase your choice of a cat or dog collar. Find the size that will fit your wrist or ankle. You could also add a charm of your choice to the buckle. This is great for girls or boys.

Luggage Labels

Add luggage tags to backpacks
or notebooks.

Bungee Cord Belts

Purchase a bungee cord in your choice of color and size to use as a belt. You could wear one, two, or even three at the same time.

Hawaiian Bracelets

To make an ankle or wrist
bracelet, pull string elastic through a
silk flower (the flower must have a small
hole); repeat to desired length. To finish, tie
a tight double knot at the end of the elastic. You
could make this a very cute headband or wear
around your neck as a lei.

Buckle Up

Cut a purchased buckle belt to the desired length for your wrist. If you need to make a hole, use a hole punch.

Tightly Wired Wristbands

Choose your favorite wire colors.
Twist one or more colors together
(see diagram 1a-c).

Hip Flops

Embellish a pair of
flip flops by attach-
ing cut yarn or rib-
bon pieces. Another
idea is to add interest to
the top of the flip-flop strap by gluing charms or colorful
earring tops (discard the back pieces of the earrings). The
dots are office supply stickers that have been attached to
the flip-flop top.

Belt It

Accessorize a leather or plastic belt with embellishments. Hot-glue a jewel onto a soda-pop cap, layered foam, or a plastic flower petal. Attach to belt.

Pack It Around

Purchase a luggage strap and wear it as a belt. Wide belt loops are necessary when you use this idea.

Pom-pom Hat

Purchase a snow hat, pom-poms in various sizes, a needle, and yarn. Thread the needle with a piece of yarn. Push the needle and yarn through the center of the pom-pom. Thread the needle through the snow hat, over the top portion, and leave up to a 3" hang; knot the yarn inside of the hat. Repeat process until your hat has the amount of pom-poms you desire. On the brim of the hat, secure pom-poms on tightly. This is a great hat in motion!

Funky Leg Warmers

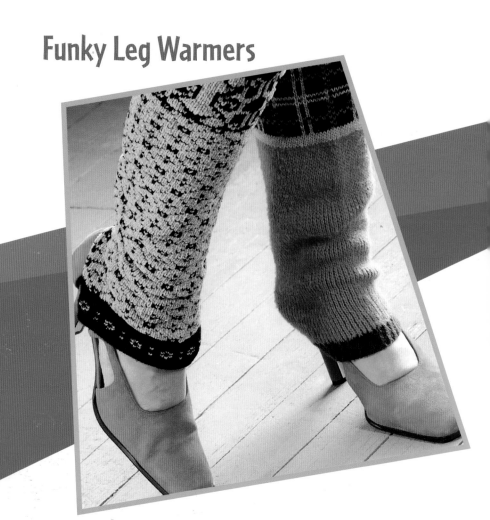

Use an old sweater that you no longer wear, or visit a local thrift shop. Cut off the sleeves (see diagram 1). You now have a great new pair of leg warmers.

Note: The rest of the sweater would make a great bag! Simply cut straight across the top and sew along the bottom edge. Use the remaining sweater scraps or add a piece of ribbon to make a handle.

1

Junky Jeans

Junk up a pair of jeans by adding flowers, iron-ons, pins, and everything but the kitchen sink. It would be a good idea to wear a simple top and let the jeans do the talking!

Bling!

Egg Carton Jewelry Box

Paint an egg carton using your favorite color of acrylic paint. This makes a nice home for all of your bling!

Pearly Girl

Make a belt using pearls. Simply add ribbon to the ends of the pearls and tie. It would also be fun to try multiple pearl belts around your waist.

Jeweled Crazy Cuffs

Purchase a plastic cuff bracelet. Attach your choice of embellishments such as jewels, beads, or old earrings with jewelry glue.

Keep your look sophisticated by letting one piece of jewelry dominate your outfit. This crazy cuff can stand alone without a lot of extra attention at your neck or fingers.

Take the chain off of any initial
necklace and attach it to ribbon instead.

Multiple Choice

You can make rings for your finger by attaching a scrapbooking letter, an earring, or any charm to a band.

Britches Bag

Make a bag from any old pair of jeans. Cut off the pant legs and sew seams where you cut the legs off. Embellish the bag with your choice of trinkets. I used vintage clip-on earrings and pretty pins. The handle is made from pearls that I bought for curtain jewelry (see page 28). I even attached the fur collar from a worn-out coat that I bought from a thrift store. This idea is so fun and quick to do. Personalize your old pair of britches to fit your style.

SECRET

You could also try this look on any lapel with multiple brooches.

Sassy

Baby Doll Cute

Purchase a baby
headband. Wrap it
two or three times
on your wrist.

An Eye for Buttons

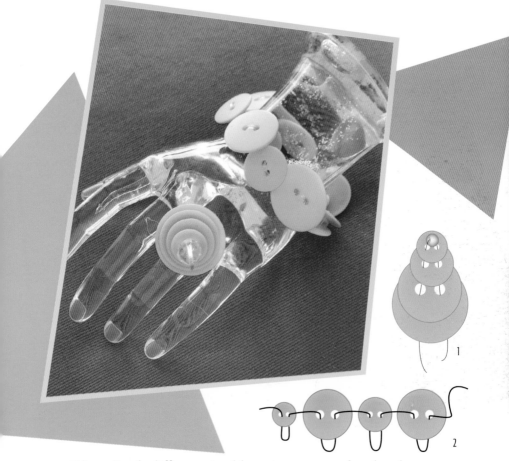

Ring: Stack different sized buttons on top of each other, starting with the larger button on the bottom. Take elastic up through the right side of the stack of buttons, add a jewel with a hole, then take elastic down through the left side (see diagram 1). Adjust to length; make a tight double knot at end. **Bracelet:** Use elastic to thread through the buttons of your choice (see diagram 2). Cut thread to desired length; make a tight double knot to end.

Decoupage Dare

Purchase clear plastic jewelry of your choice. Decoupage fabric to the inside of the plastic jewelry.

Buy a stretchy headband. Cut the headband to fit the area where you wish to wear the band. Add a polka-dot flower, charm, or earring top for embellishment.

Ring Around

Purchase a wide plastic ring. Now use craft glue to attach your favorite embellishment. This pink flower is an inexpensive earring (just pull the backing off the earring).

Feminine Finesse

Purchase two different colors of ribbon; make sure that one ribbon is wider than the other. Cut slits in the wide piece of ribbon. Weave the skinny ribbon through the wide ribbon; cut to desired length. This would be a charming choker, bracelet, hair band, or belt. The other ribbons pictured in the photo are just ribbon with an attached flower.

Soft Touch Ribbon Bracelets

Purchase ribbon, ½" belt rings, and embellishments of your choice. Sew the rings to the end of the ribbon leaving a ¼" seam; stitch the end. Attach an embellishment with fabric glue.

Pearl Piece

Add a piece of ribbon to
both ends of a string of pearls.
Wrap it around your wrist, neck, or
hair; tie together with ribbon ends.

No Boys
Allowed

Thread beads onto elastic to fit your finger. Save the large bead for the center.

Friendship Bracelets

To make a bracelet like this you will need two crimp beads, one clasp, alphabet beads, seed beads in random sizes, stretch elastic, and pliers. Slide a crimp bead on one end of the elastic and then add the clasp.

Take the end of the elastic and feed it back through the crimp bead. Close crimp bead with pliers. Randomly add seed beads, word, and more seed beads. To finish bracelet, add crimp bead and other side of clasp as before.

After School Wraps

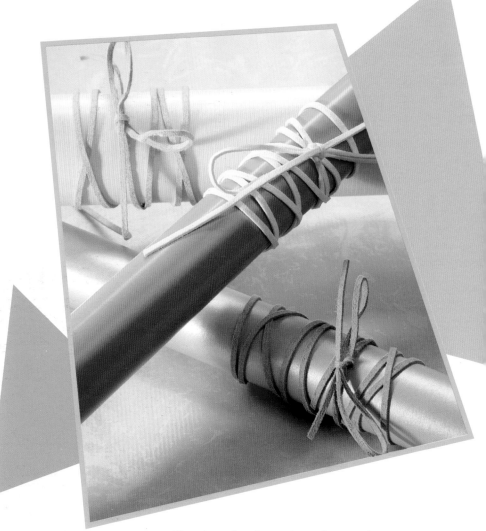

Purchase leather trim of your choice to make neck, wrist, ankle, or hair wraps. Simply wrap until you achieve the desired style.

Napkin Ring Scarves

Add a clever napkin ring
to your favorite scarf.

Shoe Style

Make a classic statement to a pair of shoes by simply adding a purchased hair bow clip. Take off the back attachment of the hair clip and glue the bow to the shoe.

Signature Initial Belts

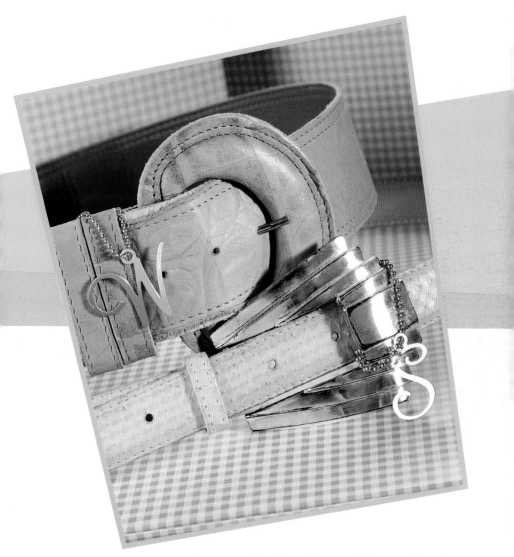

Purchase scrapbooking letters. Add your favorite letter with a small piece of chain to the belt.

Express Yourself

Purchase ribbon with words (usually found in a scrapbooking department). Wear as a wristband, neckwear, ankle bracelet, headband, or belt. You could even tie ribbon words on your backpack or key ring.

SECRET

Purchase two of the same words or expressions and give one to your friend, while you keep the other. She'll get the point.

Use fabric glue to add pom-poms or
oversized trim to a pair of socks.

Princess-cut Pillowcase Skirt

Buy a pillowcase that you love. Cut ¼" from bottom of the pillowcase (see diagram 1a). Now it's an open tube. Sew a ¼" seam. Then fold down ½" and sew (see diagram 1b). Cut a small hole in the center (see diagram 1c). Thread a drawstring through the hole; tie knots at the ends of the drawstring (see diagram 1d).

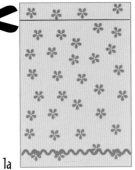

1a 1b

1c

1d

The Bright Thing

Book Clips

Use purchased hair clips to make adorable bookmarks.

These hair clips would also make hip clips to attach to a shirt, jean pocket, or even on your belt.

Just Ribbon

Tie ribbon to your neck, wrist, ankle, finger or head. Simple, but clever! You could wear just one or multiple ribbons. Personalize this look for you.

Bracelet Beads

Use elastic to thread beads on until desired wrist length. Tie into a tight double knot.

You could also use this look wrapped around your ponytail.

Clay Colors

Make your very own jewelry beads by using air-dry modeling clay. Roll your favorite colors together to make a ball. Pierce a hole through the bead, using a toothpick. Remember to make the hole big enough so that you can thread through the elastic, ribbon, or wire.

Wrist Cuffs

Buy a pair of socks.
Use a pair of scissors to
cut the seam portion of
the sock (see diagram 1a).
Cut a half inch hole for the thumb (see
diagram 1b). You can wear ragged as
shown on the right
or sew a nice clean seam to finish.

1a   1b

Plastic Party Cuffs

Purchase a plastic placemat. Cut a 2"
width and the desired length of cuff.
Attach snaps to ends for closure.

Scrapbook Bracelets

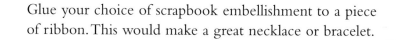

Glue your choice of scrapbook embellishment to a piece
of ribbon. This would make a great necklace or bracelet.

Purchase a fuzzy headband. Attach a
flower pin to the headband. You could use
this for a necklace, hair band, or double up for
a great bracelet.

Bright Bright Bracelets

For
a more
elegant
look, use a soft-
er color ribbon with
pastel pearls.

Just add bright ribbon
to a bright bracelet.

Charming Ribbon

Make glorious neckwear with a piece of ribbon by adding a bright charm, rhinestone, or whimsical earring (make sure that you take the back off the earring). If these colors don't work for you, take this idea and use the colors that you love.

Nice Spot

Bright Eye

Use these bright eyeglass cases as creative petite purses. They are great for holding gum, car keys, and money. These eyeglass cases were purchased as is; but you could add your own clever embellishments to any eyeglass case.

Beaded Bracelet

Use your choice of beads and a elastic string to create yourself a beautiful bracelet.

Headstand

Use fabric glue to
embellish a purchased
plastic headband with the
ribbon of your choice.

Wrap a bangle bracelet with ribbon. Use
a small dab of glue to start one end. Wrap
the ribbon around the bracelet until covered,
then glue the remaining end in place. Optional:
Add a ribbon bow for extra embellishment.

Choker Chill

Attach a small amount of boa or feather with glue to a purchased choker. You could even make a boa ring to match by simply attaching a small amount of boa to a band.

Skinny Mini Belts

For the latest look, try layering two belts together.

Attach a hair clip flower to a skinny belt.

Colorful Cuffs

Purchase a plain cuff bracelet
without embellishments. Add a simple
flower or get real creative by adding jacks (from
a dollar store "ball and jacks set"). You can also add colorful pushpins. Remove the pins on the backs, then glue
them to the cuff bracelet.

Add a flower to the top of a pair of hair or chop sticks. Attach flower with glue.

Notebook Organizers

Glue a small sequin purse to a school notebook.

This is a great way to free up your hands from so much clutter. Your change, gloss, pens, and secret stuff will be with you at a moments notice.

Sunny Sunglasses

Add extra color to your
sunglasses: paint the frame
with nail polish.

Black & White

Umbrella Chic

Produce a sassy
umbrella by adding
trim of your choice.
Make sure the trim is
weatherproof.

Mailbox Alphabets

You've got male! Purchase mailbox alphabets, then glue your favorite "male's" name to the back of your belt.

Love the Cuffs

Visit a thrift store and purchase a shirt that has cuffs for cuff links (you can choose any size). Now the fun part. Cut the cuffs off the shirt. Add a pair of cuff links–or you can use a pair of vintage clip-on earrings.

SECRET

You can even wear the shirt with cutoff cuffs ...just roll up the sleeves...sneaky stuff!

Purse Place

Add extra magic to any purse by embellishing with an accessory, like the glasses or the shiny bow that is really a hair clip. Simply remove the clip part and attach with glue.

Boa Bracelet

Glue a strip of boa
to a slap stick, using
fabric glue.

Black & White Dots

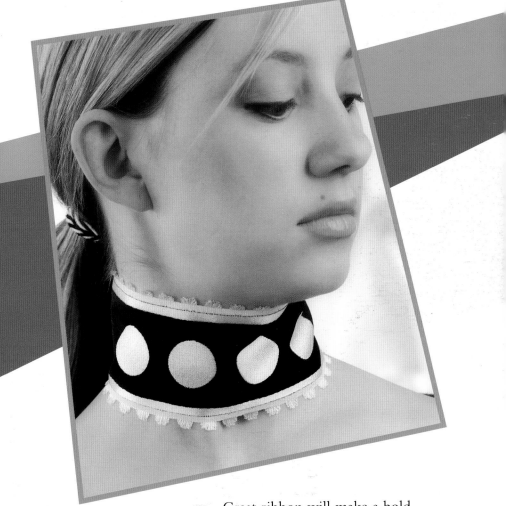

Great ribbon will make a bold
statement on your neck.

Scarf Time

Adorn a scarf with your favorite
watch or bracelet.

Standout Scarf

Use hair scrunchies to add your statement to a scarf.

Scrunchy Wrist

HOT

Use your
hair scrunchy
on your wrist.

You
will
always be
prepared with
this "always hot"
idea for any bad hair
day. The problem is: there
goes your wristwear.

Dance Hat

Add boa to the top of any knit
hat with fabric glue.

Sweet Stuff

Sassy Shoelace

Purchase a shoelace and your choice of a foam sheet. Trace and cut a flower shape on the piece of foam. Cut two slits in flower (see diagram 1). Thread the shoelace through the two holes. This makes a great belt, necklace or bracelet; it would even be fun in your hair.

1

Jump Rope Wristwear

Visit the nearest dollar store and purchase a colorful jump rope. Cut rope to the desired wrist size. Hot-glue both ends of the rope and hold ends tightly together until cool. It is also very fun to use one handle of the rope, make a tie, and then a knot on the side minus a handle.

Say It Shoelace

Purchase beads with letters on them and a great colored shoelace. Simply push shoelace through bead hole. Spell whatever sounds good to you. This makes a cute bracelet, necklace, or hair band.

You could also attach this "Say It Shoelace" to your purse, backpack, or notebook.

Pom-pom Earrings

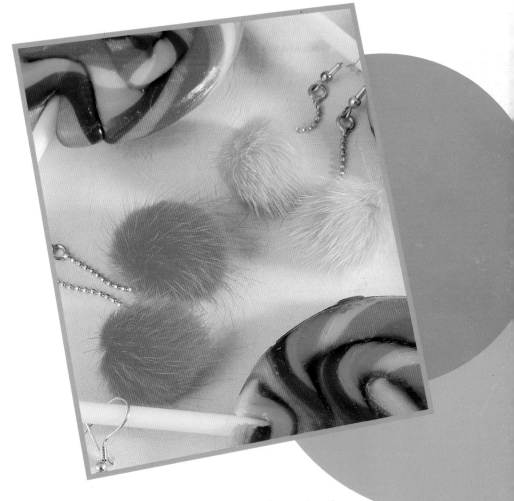

Glue small pom-poms to the ends of purchased chain earrings.

Candy Bracelet

Purchase peppermint rings and a shoelace or ribbon. Thread the peppermints onto the shoelace. Now you can have all-day fresh breath right near your fingertips.

Old-fashioned Ponytail Holders

Old-fashioned ponytail holders
make great whimsical rings. The dollar
stores always seem to have this item.

Elastic Wristwear

Instead of putting all
the elastics in your hair,
put them on your wrists.
Wear one or many.

Hidden Jewels

Make a bracelet or a ring out of pipe cleaner by simply twisting two of your favorite colors together. To make a ring out of trim, cut the trim to fit your finger, then use fabric glue to add trim embellishment like this pink flower.

Dedication

For Levi and River . . .
My loveable teenage boys.

Special Thanks to...

Laci Davis, Richard Grover, Levi
Grover, River Grover, Jarom
Johnson, Mindy Swain

About the Author

Jill Grover, an interior designer, resides with her husband and children in
Northern Utah. She has appeared locally as well as nationally on various
television programs, sharing advice on crafting and decorating. Jill is the
author of Scary Scenes for Halloween, Handmade Giftwrap, Bows, Cards,
and Tags, Dimestore Decorating, Throwing the Perfect Shower, and
Throwing the Perfect Party. She loves life, especially the energy and
inspiration she receives from the youth.

Index